Figure Skaters

Scott Hamilton

FIREWORKS ON ICE

LINDA SHAUGHNESSY

CRESTWOOD HOUSE
Parsippany, New Jersey

For my parents,
William and Betty Lou Long,
whose love of words brims over onto me

Acknowledgments

I thank the following people for helping to make this book.

Susan Lundquest, Dr. Samuel Cooper, Barbara Camp, Eleanor and Richard Powers, and Jack Carle of the *Bowling Green Sentinel-Tribune*, for their help, confidence, and trust.
Elise Feeley from Forbes Library and Pam Bowers of the BGSU Library Archives
Barb McCutcheon, J. Barry Mittan, Eleanor Powers, Susan Lundquest, Jeff Hall, Clifton Boutelle, AP/Wide World Photos, the Bettmann Archive, and the *Bowling Green Sentinel-Tribune*, for photo assistance.
William Long, the Pepin family, and Lisa Elaine Zimmerman, for video support. Sarah Dickinson, for her skating expertise and magazines. Sandra Loosemore, for her World Wide Web window into the skating world, and the rec.sport skating newsgroup.

For sharing their words: *American Skating World*, *Skating* magazine, *Tracings*, the *Boston Globe*, *Maclean's* magazine, the *Toledo Blade*, the *Bowling Green Sentinel-Tribune*, the *Bowling Green News*, Dr. Samuel Cooper, and the following sources for specific quotes.
Pages 5, 13, 15, 20, 50: Reprinted courtesy of SPORTS ILLUSTRATED 2/6/84, 2/27/84, 10/19/87, and 2/14/94 issues. Copyright © 1984, 1987, 1994 Time Inc. "Wow! Power" by Bob Ottum, "Notable Triumphs, Wrong Notes" by Bob Ottum, "Pathway to the Olympics" by Walter Bingham, and "The Killing Ground" by William Oscar Johnson. All rights reserved.
Pages 11, 12, 19, 28, 36, 39: © 1984, *The Washington Post*. Reprinted with permission.
Pages 31, 41: Time © 1984 Time Inc. Reprinted by permission.

Carol Weis, Elaine Streeter, Nancy S. Carpenter, and the Hatfield writing group. Peter, Brian and Keely, Eleanor, Mom and Dad, and the rest of my family, for both helping me on my way and calling me back home.

Photo Credits

Front cover: Barb McCutcheon: t.l., b. Sports Illustrated Picture Collection/Heinz Kluetmeir: t.r.

AP/Wide World Photos/Chris Lenney: 56. Clif Boutèlle: 15, 20. Corbis-Bettmann/UPI: 30, 34, 37, 38. Duomo: 42; David Madison: 40. Courtesy, Susan Lundquest: 9, 10, 12, 22. Barb McCutcheon: 4, 7, 45, 53. Sentinel Tribune: 17, 24, 32, 51. Sports Illustrated Picture Collection/Heinz Kluetmeir: 25, 26, 29, 33. Margaret S. Williamson: 47, 48. Glossary Illustrations: © 1998 David Uhl Studios; Ice Backgrounds © 1998 Bruce Benner Studios

Library of Congress Cataloging-in-Publication Data
Shaughnessy, Linda.
    Scott Hamilton: fireworks on ice / by Linda Shaughnessy. — 1st ed.
    p. cm. — (Figure skaters)
    Includes bibliographical references and index.

    Summary: A biography of national, world, and Olympic gold medalist figure skater Scott Hamilton.
    ISBN 0-382-39443-7 (lsb). — ISBN 0-382-39444-5 (pbk.)
    1. Hamilton, Scott, 1958– . 2. Skaters—United States—Biography.
    I. Title. II. Series.
GV850.H34S53   1998
796.91'092—dc20
[B]   96-46016

Published by Crestwood House
A Division of Simon & Schuster
299 Jefferson Road, Parsippany, NJ 07054

First Edition
Printed in the United States of America
10 9 8 7 6 5 4 3 2

CONTENTS

Audiences recognize Scott Hamilton, even under all that hair, by the way he makes them laugh.

1

MEMORIES

*It ain't much, but everything
I've got is skating muscle.*

• Scott Hamilton, to *Sports Illustrated*

The skater stood in a shower of hot lights. He wore bell-bottom pants and a vest painted with peace signs. On his head, corralled by a headband, was a towering mane of hair. As rock music blasted over the ice, he strutted, played a little air guitar, and bowed worshipfully, mocking the words of the song. Suddenly he hurled away his heap of hair and went into warp speed.

Ricocheting around the rink, he hopped and whirled like a windup toy, so fast that his blades never seemed to touch the ice. He rocketed into the air, whipped around, and landed with a punch of triumph. He spun like a high-speed drill, boring into the ice.

Beckoning to the crowd as if to say, "Hey, watch this!", he rocked forward. His legs snapped up, over, and down behind.

His blades dug in, spitting sparks of ice. The audience gasped and then cheered. It was a perfect **backflip**.

He paused, turning his vest inside out. Sticking a velcro tie to his collar on the last beat of the song, he completed the transformation from hippie to businessman. While the audience roared, Scott Hamilton stood still for once, his grin both bold and bashful.

The routine, to the title song from the musical *Hair*, was a way of poking fun at his own sandy-blond hair that was thinning on top. He performed it night after night on the 1996 Stars on Ice tour, pulling audiences to the edge of their seats and making them laugh.

It was the tenth anniversary of the tour, a time for looking back, remembering. After 28 years of skating, Scott had many memories.

One Christmas, when he was nine, he and his family visited relatives and doctors near Boston. Scott had not grown much since he was two. The specialists in Boston told the Hamiltons that he would probably live another year at the most. Searching for something to make Scott smile, his mother remembered that he had tried skating recently and had enjoyed it. She bought tickets to an ice show.

Scott had never been to a live show to see skaters performing. He loved it, especially Freddie Trenkler's act. Like Scott, Freddie was small, but he skated circles around the others. Scott laughed long and hard and felt good for a change. It was his best Christmas. He thought that if he could give that gift to others, it would make his second best Christmas.

Four months later, Scott was on the ice, delighting audiences in his hometown arena. Almost 30 years later he was still doing it, despite that prediction that he would not live another year. Through the years he had also been told that he was too small to make it to the Olympics and that male figure skaters were not popular with audiences.

He had proved them all wrong. Standing before the whooping, whistling Stars on Ice audience, Scott Hamilton had a lot to grin about.

Bell bottoms, peace signs, and hair vanish as Scott gets down to business.

ESCAPE ARTIST

Every zoo has a monkey.
• Scott Hamilton, to *American Skating World*

In October of 1958 the Hamilton family of Bowling Green, Ohio, received the call they had been waiting for. A baby boy, born on August 28, was available for them to adopt.

Dr. Ernest Hamilton taught plant ecology at Bowling Green State University (BGSU). His wife, Dorothy, was a second-grade teacher. They took their 5-year-old daughter, Susan, to Toledo to see the baby and bring him home. Susan knew all about adoption from a book her parents had given her. When she first saw her new brother, skinny and wrinkled as many babies are, she wanted to choose a different one. But she was soon so proud of him that she brought him to school for show and tell, and all the kids wanted to hold him.

Scott Scovell Hamilton could run almost as soon as he could walk and was an amazing climber. His father had to

Scott as a baby

build a cover for his crib to keep him in it. The family bought fences guaranteed to be childproof, but Scott went right over them. When he was about 2, he climbed up a ladder to the roof and was strolling along the edge before his father found him.

While cleaning one day, his mother locked all the doors and windows so that Scott could not slip outside unnoticed. When she finished her work, she looked everywhere for him, even outside. Finally she heard a giggle in the kitchen. She opened the cupboard over the refrigerator, and there he was. Another day he and the girl next door took off down the middle of the road on their tricycles to visit their dads at work. They caused quite a traffic jam.

When they thought he was old enough to understand, Scott's parents told him that he was adopted, that they had chosen him to be their child. They adopted another baby, Stephen, when Scott was about four. Before long, Stephen was bigger than Scott.

The Hamilton house was a busy place. Students and friends

Scott and his sister with part of their menagerie of pets

dropped by, and there were a lot of pets. Susan remembers that Scott was always bringing animals home. They accumulated dogs, rabbits, parakeets, alligator-like caimans, and a succession of cats named Puffy Buttons. Stephen had a pet rat, and Scott had a mynah bird that talked.

Like most brothers and sisters, the three children played and fought and got into each other's belongings. Scott enjoyed teasing and playing pranks, but no one could stay angry with him for long. He would make them laugh, and it would be all over.

In spite of the fun, Scott's parents were worried about him. They had been taking him to doctors since he was two to find out why he wasn't growing any faster. The doctors understood that he was not absorbing the food he ate. But they didn't know why. He missed more and more days of school while they searched for the answer.

3

"A FRAIL LITTLE KID"

I never really felt sick. I just felt short.
• Scott Hamilton, to *The Washington Post*

The doctors suspected that Scott's growing problem was caused by certain foods. He stopped eating foods made with wheat, such as bread, cakes, and cookies. He eliminated milk, cheese, ice cream, and other dairy products. The list grew until there was almost nothing he could eat.

Scott's mother learned to prepare new foods like jelly rolls made with rice flour. Kids teased him about the strange lunches he brought to school until they understood the reason for the special food. Sometimes they envied Scott because he was allowed to drink cola to keep up his energy. He lined up bottles of the soda on the schoolroom windowsill to cool.

Children also teased him about being adopted and about his size. He always had a snappy reply. They said he was too small to play baseball and basketball with them. He tried to

The Hamilton family, when Scott was about five years old

keep up, wanting to be good at something athletic, but he tired easily. Often he stayed in alone for recess. At home he amused himself in his room with his GI Joe army men and tanks and his collection of Matchbox cars.

He spent weeks at a time in the hospital while doctors did more tests. "They put things in my intestines and would watch on TV," he later told *The Washington Post.* "Horrible stuff."

He made friends with other sick children at the hospital, some of whom died. He learned a lot about life and death and getting along on his own. His mother came often, and he hated to see her go.

The doctors put a feeding tube into his stomach. It came out through his nose and could be hooked up to a bottle of "goop," as his sister called it. At home the bottle was hung from a pole. After the valve was opened, the chalky fluid would slowly drip in and feed him. When he was done, the tube was unhooked, draped over his cheek, and taped behind his ear.

The people of Bowling Green wondered what would become of Scott. Doctors believed they had found evidence that he had cystic fibrosis, a fatal disease. A friend of the family, Dr. Andrew Klepner, disagreed, however, and persuaded the Hamiltons to take Scott to the specialists at the Children's Hospital in Boston when they went to visit relatives at Christmas time.

Before the holidays Dr. Klepner came by the Hamilton house to take Susan skating with his daughters. A new rink had just opened at Bowling Green State University. Ernie Hamilton later told *Sports Illustrated*, "This frail little kid with the tube running across his cheek turned and said, 'You know, I think I'd like to try skating.'"

Scott later described that first time on ice. "I held onto the boards for about an hour. Then I just started skating. Skating felt natural."

The doctors in Boston confirmed that he didn't have cystic fibrosis. But they did find that part of his intestine was paralyzed, and that Scott seemed very anxious and depressed. They told the Hamiltons on Christmas Eve that Scott had a year at most to live, unless by some miracle, his intestine started working again.

Scott's mother took him to the ice show while they were in Boston to escape from their gloom. Watching Freddie Trenkler dart around the ice, making everyone roll with laughter, Scott decided that he wanted to skate like that. He wanted to make people feel good and to make a difference in their lives. It was going to make all the difference in his.

4

THE MIRACLE CURE

Find something you like to do and work hard at it.
• Scott Hamilton, to the *Bowling Green Sentinel-Tribune*

In early 1968, Scott started taking Saturday morning skating lessons. His teacher soon recognized that Scott was made for skating, just as a bird is made for flying. He had a natural understanding in his mind and body for what he was doing.

Since Bowling Green had never had a rink before, few of the townspeople knew how to skate. Instead of being smaller and slower, Scott was ahead of the crowd. He had found something athletic at which he excelled.

Glad to see Scott feeling so good about himself, his parents agreed to pay for private lessons. In the spring Scott appeared in the first Bowling Green Ice Horizons show. Though he hadn't learned many tricks yet, he looked cute and confident. The audience adored him.

There are different levels of competitive skating, like steps on a ladder. That summer, starting at the bottom—the sub-juvenile level—Scott competed for the first time. He came in second.

When the Hamilton and Klepner families were vacationing by a lake that summer, they decided to try an experiment. Dr. Klepner told Scott to eat anything he wanted. The doctor had medicine handy, in case Scott had a problem.

Scott wanted ice cream, doughnuts, and a peanut butter and jelly sandwich. After eating, he was fine. The family remained cautious after that but eventually disposed of the goop and the feeding tube, and Scott ate like everyone else.

When the Hamiltons took Scott for a checkup, they found that he had grown over an inch and had gained weight. "What have you done to this boy?" asked the doctors. "He's healthy!" They attributed the miracle to the moist, cool air in the rink and the exercise of skating.

Skating soon became part of life in the Hamilton family. Susan enjoyed being an **ice dancer** in the shows but broke her arm learning a jump from Scott. Ernie Hamilton built

In his second Ice Horizons show, ten-year-old Scott played a jack-in-the-box.

scenery and props. Dorothy made costumes and accompanied Scott to competitions. She didn't interfere with Scott's skating, but she was there when he needed her.

"She helped my confidence along by telling me to pursue short-term goals," said Scott to the *Boston Globe*. "She'd say, 'Just concentrate on bettering yourself for the little competition at hand. Don't worry about doing great things.'" He added, "She just made me feel that anything was possible."

Scott enjoyed practicing **jumps**, **spins**, and other moves that are performed to music in skating programs. He also practiced **compulsory figures** on his designated patch of ice. With certain **edges** of his skate blades, he covered the patch with huge figure eights, embellished with loops and curlicues. He pushed off hard enough on one foot to get around the circles, with his body flattened like a piece of paper. After laying out the curves, he had to trace over them exactly.

Figures did not interest Scott much though. When his teacher left Bowling Green, Scott decided he would rather play hockey. He was tired of being teased about skating with the girls. The Hamiltons were reluctant to have their 50-pound 10-year-old bashed around by bigger boys, but they let him play as long as he also continued figure skating.

Occasionally Scott got knocked out and had to be carried off the ice. But he was fast and made good use of his size, once skating between the knees of an opposing player.

In 1969, Scott won his first gold medals in figure skating at the sub-juvenile and juvenile levels. He was able to do double jumps, rotating twice in the air in his **loops, lutzes, toe loops, flips,** and **salchows.** On his first trip far from home, to California, he won a second-place trophy for his individual performance and a third place trophy in ice dancing. But his dancing career ended soon afterward. He couldn't find girls small enough to be his partner. Although he was now growing, he could never make up for the years he had lost while he was sick.

In the meantime his mother went to graduate school and started teaching home economics at BGSU. All her earnings and more went to pay for Scott's ice time, coaching, travel, costumes, and skates. She was frequently away from home with Scott at competitions. According to Scott, he was spoiled, but others deny it.

He did well in school and brought his homework when he went away to compete. He was likable and charming, despite the pranks he liked to play. One time he shot fireworks from the roof of the ice arena. When the campus police finally

Between hockey and figure skating, Scott spent a lot of time at the rink.

17

caught him, he talked himself out of trouble and even got to keep the fireworks.

By the time Scott was 12, he had passed tests in the first two levels of figures. But he failed the third level test three times, twice so badly that the judges stopped him in the middle. He finally passed, however, and advanced to the intermediate level. At a regional competition two weeks later, he came in first in figures and then won overall.

Newspaper reporters had been writing about him as the sick little boy who was cured by skating. But now they spread the news that Scott Hamilton was an exciting talent to watch.

5

A Rough
Patch

The only thing he took seriously
was having a good time.
• *The Washington Post*

By the time he was 13, Scott realized that he was aiming for the top—the **World Championships** and the Olympics. His parents knew that he needed more training than he could get in Bowling Green.

They found a resort called the Wagon Wheel, north of Chicago, where Janet Lynn, the heart-warming five-time United States champion, had trained. Scott spent more and more time there, working with a coach named Pierre Brunet, until at 15, he was living and training there year-round.

Scott got along well with Monsieur Brunet. The Frenchman took apart everything Scott knew and made him learn it again. Brunet's specialty was figures. He taught Scott that if he positioned his body the right way, correct tracings on the ice would follow.

After leaving home to train, Scott returned to guest star in Ice Horizons shows.

United States champion Gordie McKellen was also training at the Wagon Wheel. Like Scott, Gordie was compact and had a style that was athletic rather than like ballet on skates.

Gordie showed Scott how to handle himself on and off the ice. Living in the dormitory at the Wagon Wheel was like being at yearlong summer camp. Scott joined in on the pranks and partying. "I liked girls and dating but didn't take skating seriously," Scott later told *Sports Illustrated.*

In 1974, vaulting from a top bunk, Scott shattered his ankle. As soon as it was out of the cast, he was competing again and winning, but his ankle looked and felt terrible.

And then came the news that his mother had breast cancer. She had surgery, but the cancer spread to other parts of her body. Yet she continued to teach and join Scott at competitions when she felt well enough.

In 1975, Scott competed at the National Championships against the best junior skaters in the United States. There were three parts to competitions: compulsory figures; the technical, or **short program**; and the freestyle, or **long program**. His figures were good, and his technical program with required jumps and spins and **footwork** was excellent. But nervousness hindered his freestyle program. When his placements for all three parts were figured together, he ended up in seventh place overall.

That year Pierre Brunet retired from coaching. It looked as though Scott was also at the end of his career. The Hamiltons had no more money for skating. Scott made plans to go to college in Bowling Green in the fall and prepared to compete one last time as a junior at the 1976 **Nationals**.

He did well in the figures and technical parts of the competition. But the night of the freestyle, his last performance, Scott was downhearted. Fearing that his mood would affect his skating, his mother told him the news that she had planned to save until after the competition. A wealthy couple had offered to pay all of Scott's expenses for as long as he wanted to skate.

Feeling much better, Scott skated a winning performance. He became the United States Junior Champion! On the way home he met the couple who wanted to sponsor him. They soon felt like family to him.

Scott moved to Denver to train at the Colorado Ice Arena with Carlo Fassi. Fassi had just coached Dorothy Hamill and John Curry to gold medals at the 1976 Olympics. Scott lived with a Denver family, in the same room Dorothy Hamill had used. He suspected that she had kept it neater than he did. Between practices, he completed his school work,

Dorothy Hamilton,
Scott's mother

enabling him to graduate in June from the high school in Bowling Green.

At the time, he told the *Bowling Green News* that he didn't want to depend on skating for his living. "There's not a lot of money in professional skating—not for a guy," he said.

That summer Scott moved into an apartment and bought a car. He passed his final figures test. At last he could skate at the senior level, the top. He competed in Europe for the first time, coming in second and third in competitions in Germany and France. It was as if he were at the peak of a roller coaster and the world was his. Then he plunged downward.

Because of injury and lack of focus, his 1977 season was disappointing. He finished ninth at his first senior Nationals, the last competition that his mother saw. Despite the treatments and surgery, her cancer was overtaking her. On May 19, 1977, Dorothy Hamilton died.

Scott wouldn't talk to anyone. His mother had done so much for him. And he felt that he had repaid her by fooling around instead of working hard.

He remembered how she had told her friends, while they played cards and bragged about their children, that Scott was going to the Olympics. Scott decided that from then on, he would skate for her and make her vision come true.

6

KEEPING HIS
VOW

You train like there's no tomorrow and, at the final moment, you have to let all that's in you happen.

• Scott Hamilton, to the *Boston Globe*

Unlike most skaters, Scott excelled in both figures and freestyle skating. At the 1978 senior Nationals, he came in third, behind reigning United States champion Charlie Tickner and David Santee.

Finishing in the top three at Nationals meant that he could represent the United States at his first World Championships. Competing in Ottawa, Canada, against the best skaters in the world, 19-year-old Scott finished respectably, in eleventh place.

But the 1979 season was a struggle. Scott injured the ankle on which he landed his jumps. He was unhappy with his coach. And at Nationals, despite good performances, he finished out of the top three. The closest he got to the World Championships was to watch on TV. He vowed not to be left out again.

Finishing the 1979 Nationals without a medal, Scott turned disappointment into determination.

He packed up and drove east to find a new coach, winding up at the Philadelphia Skating Club and Humane Society where Don Laws, a former National Champion, had taught skating for over twenty years. Laws saw that Scott could go far if he worked hard. Scott was ready and willing.

Rooming with a large family that lived nearby, Scott fit right in. He drove off early in the morning in his noisy red MG sports car to practice at the rink. At lunchtime he returned, watched soap operas, and relaxed. From 4:00 to 7:00 he practiced again and then came home for supper. He had no particular training diet and liked almost everything, especially chicken mushroom casserole.

After supper Scott played card games like hearts with the family until bedtime. He delivered pizzas for pocket money for a while, but that didn't work out because he had to take so much time off to go to competitions. He spent the little spare time that he had with friends like Kitty and Peter Carruthers, **pairs skaters** who trained in nearby Delaware. Like Scott, they had also been adopted.

Before competitions, for good luck his friends gave him mushrooms made of ceramics, metal, or wood to add to his collection. For a while Scott also felt that eating a chicken sandwich before competing would bring him luck.

While waiting to skate, he listened to loud rock music and focused on his program. He paced at the rink, trying to convince himself that he was going to do well. It was part of his process.

Scott worked for clean body lines that made his body appear longer.

Laws understood Scott's process. He was a teacher, father, brother, and friend, depending on what Scott needed. Scott worked harder than ever, fine-tuning every movement and position. His triple jumps were high and consistently landed. The speed of his footwork was incredible. Even Laws couldn't explain how Scott did it.

Aerial acrobatics

Two triples eluded him—the loop and the **axel**. The axel was three and a half turns in the air. One day he'd land it, but the next day he wouldn't quite make it around. In the autumn of 1979, at the Flaming Leaves international competition at Lake Placid, Scott finished fourth in figures. He won the technical program and finished with a dazzling freestyle program to win overall. It was a great beginning to the 1980 Olympic season.

At the Nationals in January, finishing in third place again behind Tickner and Santee, Scott qualified for the Olympic team. His mother had been right—he was going to the Olympics!

In Lake Placid the athletes on the United States Olympic team voted to give Scott the honor of carrying the flag in the opening ceremonies. In shock, he treated them to coffee in the cafeteria and spilled the hot beverage all over his hands! But he was steady with the flag, beaming under the rim of a cowboy hat three sizes too big. It was one of his proudest moments.

He felt nervous about skating in front of the worldwide Olympic audience, but he knew that no one expected him to win. He hoped to finish in the top five. When the time came, Scott skated a great long program and ended up in fifth place overall. He was fifth again at the World Championships a month later.

Bowling Green held a dinner to honor Scott and two members of the United States hockey team. Scott thanked the people of his hometown for their support. After skating in a tour of champions, he returned to Bowling Green to perform in their International Stars on Ice show.

The show was a benefit to raise money for the American Cancer Society in memory of his mother. It would be repeated every other year, alternating with the Ice Horizons show. Ernie Hamilton was proud of the way Scott was using his talent to help others.

Like a silver ball in a pinball machine, Scott had sprung into the flash and zap of top-level skating. When Robin Cousins retired after winning at the 1980 Olympics, he told Scott that the next Olympic gold medal would be his, if he wanted it. But the next Olympics was four years away. Could Scott stay in play that long?

7

PEAKS AND VALLEYS

In 1978, a judge said because of my size I'd never be taken seriously internationally. He said, "Nobody will ever mark you up. No one will consider you a man because you'll always look like a boy."
• Scott Hamilton, to *The Washington Post*

When the Colorado Ice Arena had an opening for a coach, Don Laws decided to take it. Scott went with him, back to Denver and Dorothy Hamill's old room. They began work on new programs for the 1981 season.

Scott felt that if skating were more like sport than dance, it would reach a bigger audience. Skating was "not just for people who have a taste for artistry," he told *Skating* magazine. "It's something that everybody can enjoy."

He looked for ways to show that with his music, his choreography, and his costume. Though he had nothing against the spangles men wore on their costumes, he wanted something simple that would accent the lines he was making with his body.

After listening to hundreds of dollars' worth of music, Scott, Laws, and choreographer Ricky Harris chose pieces with contrasting styles and moods. They cleverly patched the pieces together and programmed movements to them according to their "Wow! Wow! Wow!" theory.

"Start with some technical stuff to show them you're proficient," Scott explained to the *Bowling Green News*. "Then let them have something dramatic. They jump out of their seats."

The 1981 Nationals were in San Diego, California. Ernie Hamilton was there to watch his son battle for the gold medal. On the morning of the short program, Ernie awoke to the ringing of the telephone, but he could not raise his arm to answer it. He had suffered a stroke. He concealed the problem from Scott not wanting to worry him. On the night of the long program, Ernie wished Scott good luck and then went to the hospital.

Coach Don Laws and Scott fine-tune each position and movement.

David Santee of the U.S. and Igor Bobrin of the USSR share the podium with the 1981 world champion, Scott Hamilton.

He was admitted but refused to be sedated until Scott burst into his room with a gold medal—the new United States Champion!

Scott wondered why very good things and very bad things seemed to follow closely in his life. Remaining with his father until Ernie was able to go home, Scott considered skipping the 1981 World Championships in Hartford just a few weeks away. When he finally decided to go, there was little time to train.

In third place going into the freestyle program, 22-year-old Scott glided out in front of a sellout crowd of 14,600 fans. Though he was only 5 feet 3 ½ inches tall, his presence was huge. He skated brilliantly except for one fall while gathering speed for a jump. The crowd gave him a standing ovation, and the judges gave him high scores, including several 5.9's, out of a perfect 6.0.

Scott Hamilton was the champion of the world.

8

CHAIN OF GOLD

I realized that I didn't have to be what the champions before me had been. I could be me.

• Scott Hamilton, to *Time* magazine

Bowling Green claimed the new world champion as its own, putting Scott's name on signs at the entrances to the city. On the tour of champions after Worlds, Scott needed no introduction when he stepped onto the ice. His country was proud of him.

But becoming world champion was like moving into an unfamiliar neighborhood. What would people expect of him? What should he expect of himself?

It was a hard year. He felt that audiences didn't recognize how difficult it was to stay on top. He couldn't win them over or surprise and excite them the way he had the first time. When he won competitions, it felt more like "not losing"; he felt more relief than satisfaction. "I drove myself crazy," he said later to *Time* magazine. "I was terrible to myself and everyone around me."

Frequently interviewed for TV and newspapers, Scott usually knew what to say.

In 1982 he won the United States Nationals and the Worlds again. Scott had won gold in his last eight competitions. He began to feel pressure from being undefeated for so long.

Scott was often interviewed and featured on television. He was courted by agents hoping to sign him as their client. He appeared at benefits for charities and skated in exhibitions to promote his sport.

CBS TV, impressed with how quick Scott was with words, hired him to do the commentary during their skating events. The first time he tried it, he found it was hard to know what to say and to remember to look at the camera. But he worked at it, thinking of his future. Broadcasting was a way to make a living after retiring from skating.

Scott strove to find enough time to train. Other skaters

were working on triple axels, more difficult **combination jumps**, **quadruple jumps**, and new styles of artistry. Scott wanted to develop his own skills and prepare fresh, new programs for the coming 1983 season.

He unveiled his new costume design. It was blue, one piece, and snug in fit, like a speed-skater's outfit. Scott felt great just putting it on. His choreography, like his costume, lacked the frills that European skaters seemed to prefer. Scott called his style "apple pies and Chevrolets."

His music was a sequence of crackling synthesizer sounds, modern jazz, and haunting Asian melodies, with a bit of a waltz thrown in to startle and amuse. Humor was risky. The judges might not consider it appropriate for competition. But Scott wanted his program to stand out. And he had never forgotten how good he had felt long ago watching funny Freddie Trenkler.

The risk paid off—Scott claimed the 1983 national title. He competed in his new costume for the first time at the World Championships in Helsinki, Finland. Placing second in figures, he moved into first place with a strong technical

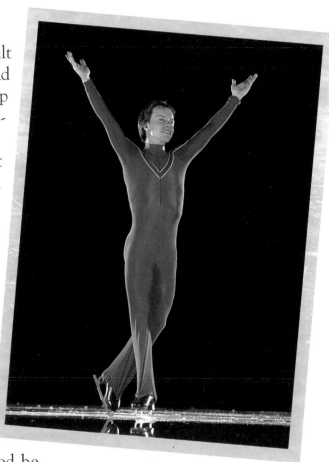

Scott preferred a simple design so that the full effect of his skating could be seen.

At the 1984 National Championships, Scott received four perfect scores for his artistic presentation.

program. He began his long program with a stunning triple lutz/triple toe loop combination jump and sailed through the rest. For the first time in 24 years, a skater from the United States had won three consecutive World Championships.

Since first becoming world champion, he had grown into his talent and had become a man. He liked who he was and appreciated his size, so perfect for skating. He trusted himself. "I understand that it's not an accident if I skate well, that if I want to, I can," he told *Skating* magazine.

The 1984 National Championships in Salt Lake City were a glorious send-off for Scott and a strong message to his Olympic competitors. Judges gave Scott 45 scores that week, and every one was first place. He got four marks of 6.0

for artistic presentation, bringing his career total of perfect scores to 8.

Most people expected Scott to win the gold medal at the 1984 Olympics in Sarajevo in February. The pressure was enormous. No wonder Scott's hair was thinning out!

In Bowling Green the Rotary Club held a dinner to raise $2,000 for Ernie Hamilton to go to Sarajevo. Many friends were going, too. Kitty and Peter Carruthers, Elaine Zayak, Rosalynn Sumners, and Judy Blumberg and Michael Seibert had come up the ladder with Scott. As part of the Olympic team, they would share with him the moments they had awaited so long. Whatever happened in Sarajevo, their wait would soon be over. It would be time for a new dream when they came home.

At 25, Scott had been waiting longer than most of the other athletes. He was not just hoping to win. He wanted the Olympics to be the greatest performance of his life.

9

SARAJEVO

*This is the goose bump competition
to end goose bump competitions.*
• S c o t t   H a m i l t o n ,   t o   *T h e   W a s h i n g t o n   P o s t*

Sarajevo is in a bowl of a valley, surrounded by mountains, in the middle of the former country of Yugoslavia. It snowed a lot that February, making the industrial city look clean and white. There were handsome, centuries-old mosques and museums built by Serbs, Muslims, Croats, and other peoples who had lived there.

Under Communist rule at the time, Sarajevan citizens had to provide help at the Olympics for those two weeks, and they did so with warmth and pride. One day, workers tried to sweep snow from the outdoor speed-skating rink while more was falling. They gave up and made snow angels.

After a private week of practice in Paris, Scott arrived for the opening ceremonies. He had caught a little cold, but he was skating very well. There was more than a week to wait before the start of the men's skating competition. Scott practiced in Zetra Arena for an hour and a half each day and then watched the skiing and other events. He was hounded by reporters wanting photographs and interviews.

On a Monday morning the compulsory figures began. Scott attempted the first figure in front of the line of judges. The judges brushed the snow away and scrutinized the tracing, their noses almost to the ice. They recorded their score and called the next skater to begin. Scott had a nerve-racking wait for his turn to do the second figure, and then the third one.

Even as a spectator at the other Olympic events, Scott was entertaining.

For the first time in international competition, Scott came in first in all three figures and won overall, something he had hoped to do before retiring. Since figures were worth

Placing first in figures gave Scott a big lead, and, for the first time, he needed it.

30 percent of the total score, Scott had made a great start.

The next day, as he warmed up for the short program, he heard fans screaming his name from the stands. Suddenly he felt shaky. His jumps felt strange. At the end of warm-up, he went down into the basement and scolded himself for watching the other Olympic events. He had lost his focus.

Skating his program, Scott had trouble lifting off into the jumps. His **camel** spin bothered him. He felt as if he were skating in slow motion, and he almost crashed once into the boards surrounding the rink.

Even so, he came in second in the short program, behind Canadian Brian Orser. But Orser had come in seventh in figures. The way the numbers worked out, Scott would have to finish in fifth place or worse in the long program to lose the gold medal.

Thursday night 6,500 boisterous spectators filled Zetra Arena. Scott thought the Americans in the crowd sounded like hockey fans. "They were yelling 'Kill 'em! Go get 'em!'" he said. He was glad they were there.

Pacing downstairs while Orser skated, Scott could hear the crowd's wild applause. When Scott glided onto the ice, he picked up a few roses that fans had thrown for Brian. He stroked to his starting position. Everything he had done for the last 16 years had led to this moment. His music blasted out like laser light, and he sprang into action.

He felt as if he had 20-pound weights on his ankles. Struggling to stay straight in the air, he landed a triple lutz, triple toe loop, a triple/double combination jump and two double axels. He came down from his triple salchow after only two revolutions, and his triple flip turned out to be a single. His footwork and spins were good, though not up to his usual precision. The spectators were on their feet with a thunderous ovation before he had finished. But Scott wished he could restart the music and try it again.

"I'm sorry," he said as he came off the ice.

Don Laws told the *Boston Globe*, "I think the excitement, the buildup over four years, just swelled up inside Scott." He also revealed that Scott's cold had developed into an ear infection, which was affecting his sense of balance and how he felt in the air.

Brian Orser won the long program, with Scott taking second. But when the overall scores were tallied, Scott Hamilton had won the highest honor in amateur figure skating, the Olympic gold medal.

The new Olympic champion carries the flag in another proud moment.

Scott stood on the top tier of the podium. Tears rolled down his face as "The Star-Spangled Banner" played. He had never even seen an Olympic gold medal, and now he had one hanging around his neck. He had wanted it to be a moment to remember, and it was, though not quite the way he had planned.

He charged around the rink for the victory lap, waving and smiling, followed by silver medalist Brian Orser and bronze medalist Josef Sabovcik of Czechoslovakia. As the gate opened for them to step off the ice, Scott snatched a huge United States flag from a spectator. With it unfurled and fluttering behind him, he led the medalists one more time around.

10

UNFINISHED
BUSINESS

To know Scott Hamilton is to know that nice guys do finish first. There's probably nothing he can't do.
• Don Laws, to the *Bowling Green Sentinel-Tribune*

To the American people, Scott was a hero. President Reagan called to congratulate him and invite him to the White House. The New York Yankees asked him to throw out the first baseball of their season. In Bowling Green the signs at the city limits were updated with his Olympic achievement, and a street was named after him.

"Maybe it wasn't pretty, but I did it," Scott told reporters. He felt proud, but he was glad that he had another chance, at the World Championships, to deliver the performance he knew he could do.

The 1984 Worlds were in Ottawa, Canada, where his first Worlds had been. He felt 100 pounds lighter without the Olympic pressure. He won the figures and the short program. Though Brian Orser took the long program, Scott

President and Mrs. Reagan welcomed Scott to the White House.

held him off again from winning overall. It was his fourth world championship and his eighteenth gold medal in a row.

After Worlds he seriously considered what his next step would be. Scott had a sense of unfinished business, of great performances yet to happen and more to do for the sport. But for 16 years he had lived according to rink schedules and competition calendars. Despite intense pressure, he had won everything he had set out to win. At the end of March, Scott officially announced his retirement from amateur skating.

He had already picked out nice living quarters in a Denver high-rise building with a view of the mountains. He liked Denver, with its western "cowboy" feeling. The city celebrated his victories by parading him around on an antique fire engine. He was presented with gifts, including a 200-pound, orange-capped fire hydrant.

The townspeople of Bowling Green had made special plans for Scott's visit in May to do the International Stars on Ice show. He was paraded from school to school, where students gave him gifts and asked questions.

They asked about his gold medal, his childhood, and his

plans for the future. "I'm looking for a job," he told them. "If you know of one, write and let me know."

"It was the best thing they could have done, to gear it toward kids," he said about the day to the *Bowling Green Sentinel-Tribune*. "Kids are everything."

At a gathering in the evening, Scott was presented with more gifts and a check for the new Dorothy Hamilton Memorial Fund, to benefit cancer victims. He spoke about how cancer touched the lives of everybody, and how by skating he hoped to be a factor in wiping out the disease.

At the ice show that year Scott, Kitty and Peter Carruthers, and Rosalynn Sumners performed as amateurs for the last time. At the end Scott pulled his gold medal from inside his costume to show everyone what they had helped him to accomplish. Some thought that he was holding it up for one person especially—his mother.

And then he began his new life. He chose agents to handle the requests for his time and attention. He joined the teaching staff of the Colorado Ice Arena and thought about going to college. CBS continued to give him broadcasting assignments. His golf game improved.

At the end of the summer, Scott joined the Ice Capades. It was very different from amateur skating. Now he shared the ice with Smurfs and other cartoon characters. Performing was fun, but the schedule was grueling, with two or three shows a day and frequent travel from city to city. Injured or not, he was expected to go out and do his job. The applause was pleasing, but was no substitute for winning a new title every year. He felt he wasn't being challenged to improve as a skater, although he did learn a new trick—the backflip.

A gymnastics movement, the backflip was not allowed in amateur figure-skating competition. Greg Weiss, Olympic gymnast and father of skater Michael Weiss, taught Scott the dangerous maneuver. Scott claimed that it was the hardest jump to learn and the easiest to do. If his legs didn't get all the way over, the consequences could be disastrous.

Then in 1986 the Ice Capades managers told Scott they weren't renewing his contract. They said that audiences weren't interested in watching male skaters. Two years after winning his Olympic gold medal, Scott seemed to be old news.

At a Florida beach soon afterward, he and his agent and friend, Bob Kain, talked about what to do next. Scott missed the challenge of pushing himself to skate better. He thought there should be a show for skaters who wanted to improve their skill and artistry instead of becoming museum pieces like their medals. They could create their own programs for audiences that came to see quality skating.

It sounded like a good idea to Kain. They decided to give it a try.

Scott dives backward into a backflip, his trademark move.

11

THE SCOTT HAMILTON AMERICA TOUR

*People used to figure you turn pro, join a show,
make money, and fade off into the distance.
Things aren't like that anymore.*

• Scott Hamilton, to *American Skating World*

In the fall of 1986, the Scott Hamilton America Tour visited five New England college towns. The nine-member cast included champions Rosalynn Sumners, and Toller Cranston.

There was no glitz, no cartoon characters, no fancy scenery. The artistic skating set the mood and fired the imagination. In addition to solo performances, the cast joined together for a skit about sailors on leave from their ship. It was creative and funny, and audiences loved it.

In the finale of the first show in Orono, Maine, the spotlight cable blew up, showering the skaters with sparks and smoke. The audience thought it was part of the show until the ambulances arrived. The show traveled on, and the tour was a success.

In December, Scott and Bob Kain put together another tour, this time including Dorothy Hamill and Robin Cousins. The tour provided a place to practice in front of an audience for the few professional competitions coming up.

The competitive spirit was still strong in Scott. In the World Professional Championships in 1985, Robin Cousins had narrowly defeated him, but in 1986 Scott was the winner. He was feeling better about his skating. His jumps were solid and consistent. He had new footwork and moves that took hard work to get right. He was learning many new programs, each like a different character or personality inside of him. Fortunately, when the music started, he knew which one to be.

In 1987, Scott toured with Festival on Ice, a show

Skating as a professional, Scott became more creative with his costumes.

Scott's Battle Hymn of the Republic program was dedicated to the U.S. Figure Skating Team, which perished in a plane crash in 1961.

performed in theaters on a portable, stage-sized rink. In Broadway on Ice musicals, he tried acting as well as skating and got good reviews. Sea World in California asked him to produce a couple of ice shows at their resort.

The America tour got a sponsor and a new name—the Discover Card Stars on Ice. Dorothy Hamill stayed with the show as it toured 13 cities across the country. In 1988, when several Olympic champions retired, many wanted to continue their careers in a show like Stars on Ice. Scott had started something new, and it had caught on.

OFF-ICE AMBASSADOR

*It's not so much what you do when
you're in sports but how you leave it,
if you changed it or left something.*

• Scott Hamilton, to *Skating* magazine

In 1990, Scott Hamilton was inducted into the United States Olympic Hall of Fame and the World Figure Skating Hall of Fame. He continued to receive honors and awards, for his skating and for what he was doing behind the scenes to help the sport.

People went to him for answers and opinions. He kept informed about amateur skating as preparation for his TV commentary and because he cared about what was happening in the sport. He donated his medals, costumes, and old skates to the World Figure Skating Museum in Colorado.

Remembering his own childhood, Scott made time for kids. He sometimes kept the tour bus waiting while he signed autographs and talked with them. The Stars on Ice tour raised money for the Make-A-Wish Foundation, which grants the wishes of sick children who have little chance of recovery. Scott also raised funds for Athletes Against Drugs, pediatric AIDS, and children's hospitals.

In his commentary for the 1992 Olympics in Albertville, France, Scott found positive things to say about each performance, even if there were many falls. He understood how anybody could have a bad day.

As the 1994 Olympics approached, Scott commented on something other than skating—Sarajevo. In the ten years since Scott had won his gold medal there, the Communist hold over Yugoslavia had ended. Serbs, Muslims, and Croats were at war with one another, some committing unbelievably cruel acts. Parts of Sarajevo had been destroyed. The speed skating rink was pocked with bomb craters. Zetra Arena and other Olympic sites were in ruins or being used as military quarters.

Scott joined other athletes in efforts to bring relief to the war-torn region. Scott told *Sports Illustrated*, "For me those 13 days are always going to be my best 13 days. If I ever have grandchildren, those will be the 13 days. . . they'll ask me about. But what's happening now doesn't make any sense to me. It's all so devastating, and you wonder about the people, the volunteers, who gave us so much then."

While doing the commentary on the last day of the 1994 Olympics in Lillehammer, Scott received shocking news. His father had died.

Although Ernie Hamilton had not been well for a few years, his death was unexpected. Scott fought through departing Olympic crowds to get a flight to Florida, where Ernie had been living. After the funeral in Bowling Green, Scott flew to New York to do the Stars on Ice show that evening at Madison Square Garden. Somehow he got through it, imagining that his father was there as usual, sharing it with him.

Gentle Ernest Hamilton was missed by many people. One of them was Dr. Sam Cooper, who had been Ernie's friend, and Scott's, for many years. Scott had known Sam since they had started skating in Bowling Green, Sam at age 55 and Scott at 9. "I was better than Scott for about six or eight weeks," said Sam. They still skated together, performing "Me and My Shadow," with Sam in a white tuxedo and Scott in black. "If I stumble, Scott stumbles," said Sam. "It all works out."

That spring Sam nominated Scott for an honorary doctoral degree in performing arts from Bowling Green State University. In May, Sam placed the special hood around Scott's neck and pronounced him "Dr. Hamilton." It was a great moment for both of them.

In the cold rain that day, Scott also gave a speech packed with humor and sound advice to the graduating class. When he finished, the students held up score cards, judging his speech.

Ernie Hamilton had always enjoyed attending Scott's performances.

13

IN
DEMAND

*The shows are easy. Getting from
city to city is the hard part.*

• Scott Hamilton, to *Maclean's* magazine

By the mid-1990s, figure skating was the second most popular
sport on TV, behind football. There were all kinds of skating
shows. If Scott wasn't performing in them, he was doing
the commentary.

He skated in Halloween and Christmas specials and played
all seven dwarfs in a Disney show. He was in Skates of Gold,
an exhibition of Olympic gold medalists. He had a skating
duel with Elvis Stojko on *Too Hot to Skate*. He did some
incredible sock-skating in the kitchen on the comedy show
Roseanne and demonstrated the forces of spinning on the
science show *Newton's Apple*.

Many of the new shows were competitions. Scott was used
to pleasing audiences, not judges. With the help of coach
Kathy Casey, he prepared to compete against champions

such as athletic Brian Boitano, classy Viktor Petrenko, dramatic Paul Wylie, and the new kid on the professional block, Kurt Browning. Scott knew he couldn't expect to win all the time. But he tried.

The rules for each competition varied. The judging varied, too. Some competitions used skating experts as judges. Some used celebrities with a good sense of what was entertaining. At the Great Skate Debate, the entire audience had black boxes to enter their scores for each skater. Scott won them over with a stunning triple lutz and the stripes of lights blinking down his pant legs at the end of his program.

It made sense to him to let the audience express opinions. That was who he skated for, every time he stepped onto the ice.

"If I come in fourth and I get a standing ovation, I am the happiest guy in the world," he told *American Skating World*.

When Scott reaches out with his humor, the audience can't resist.

"If I come in first and someone else got a better reaction, I want to get the reaction that the other guy got."

With the boom in skating shows, it became possible for skaters to earn a comfortable living on the ice. One season Scott earned over a million dollars from competitions alone.

But some people felt that professional skating competitions, like professional wrestling matches, were mostly for show. A governing body was needed to organize the events into a schedule and to set rules for competitions and standards for judging. Scott did whatever he could to establish professional skating as a legitimate sport.

14

Rink Master

*He tells anyone willing to listen that he has lost his legs,
his jumps, his timing. Then he goes out and nails
everything, including 6 backflips a night....
he still has the fastest feet in the business....*

• *Maclean's* magazine

The 1995-1996 Stars on Ice show began with a spotlight on Scott, wearing gleaming white from head to toe pick. Like a seagull in the hot sun, he flew into motion. His widespread arms seemed to gather the audience in, as if to say "Come play!"

Other skaters, also in white, joined him. Over the years the cast had changed, with Rosalynn Sumners and Scott being the only original members left. Traveling on the road together to 55 cities in four or five months, the cast became a family. At 37, Scott felt like the father of the group. He had a T-shirt that said, "The older I get, the better I was."

The tenth anniversary show was about remembering. The skaters in white gazed for a moment at the spot where pairs champions Ekaterina Gordeeva and Sergei Grinkov would

Scott enjoyed making Sergei laugh.

have stood. In November, while practicing for the opening night in Lake Placid, 28-year-old Sergei had died of a heart attack. The gentle Russian's friendship and love for life had warmed them all. The skaters remembered, every night.

Later in the show, after Scott's *Hair* routine, melancholy music floated throughout the arena. Scott skated as if everyone had gone home and he was wrapping up the day with his old friend, the ice.

At one point he dragged his blade with a sound like a long sigh and scooped up the snow he had made. He cupped his hand around a make-believe glass and tossed the snow like an icecube into it. He raised the glass, and his eyes, in a private toast to someone special.

He had had a lot of special people in his life—his father, his mother, and Sergei, among others. He was grateful for their love and support. But there had been no shortcuts through the hours of practice or up the steps of the ladder. Scott had earned everything that he had accomplished.

"It is his commitment, dedication, and persistence, as well as his talent, that see him through," said Sam Cooper. "He hangs on and works like heck!"

Scott was still working on his triple axel. He once said that he planned to do less but would never retire. As long as his triples were consistent and the applause when he finished was louder than when he started, he would skate.

He told the audience of Stars on Ice, ". . . there's not a place on earth I would rather be . . . than out there on this surface of ice sharing this evening with all of you."

It was a gift he was still passing on.

GLOSSARY

axel
A jump with a forward take-off on the outside edge of one skate, rotation(s), and an extra half-turn to land on the back outside edge of the opposite skate.

backflip
A gymnastic move from a backward glide, flipping the legs up and back over the head and landing on one or two feet.

camel
A one-foot spin with the body and other leg in a horizontal position.

combination jump
One jump followed by another, with no steps or turns between.

compulsory figures, figures
Patterns that are drawn and traced on the ice with certain edges of skate blades. Early "figure" skaters, in the late 1800s, could do elaborate designs. In competition, figures were worth 50 percent of a skater's score until 1973, when the technical program was added. Cut to 30 percent and then 20 percent, figures were finally eliminated from competition in 1991.

edge
The sharp inside or outside rim of the blade of a skate.

flip
A jump from the back inside edge of the skate, boosted by the toe of the other foot from behind. After rotating, the landing is on the back outside edge of the other skate (the boosting foot).

footwork
A series of quick steps, turns, and changes of edge.

ice dancer
A skater who, with a partner, performs routines requiring dance elements, almost constant contact, and no lifts above the waist.

jump
Any of the various ways of leaping into a spin in the air and landing. The turns can be single, double, triple, or quadruple.

long program
The second part of a competition, also called the freestyle program, lasting 4 or 4 1/2 minutes, and showing the skater's best skills and artistry.

loop
A jump taking off backward from an outside edge and landing in a backward direction on the same edge.

lutz

A jump, taking off from a long glide backward on the outside edge of one skate, with a boost from behind from the other toe. The backward landing is on the outside edge of the opposite (boosting) skate.

Nationals

The yearly competition held in January or February to determine the champions who will represent a country at the World Championships and Olympics.

pairs skater

One of two partners skating in harmony and performing routines, including spins, jumps, high lifts, and throws.

quadruple jump, quad

A jump with a spin of 4 rotations, or 4 $\frac{1}{2}$ for a quad axel.

salchow (sou cou)

A jump starting from a back inside edge, landing backward on the outside edge of the opposite skate.

short program

The first part of a competition, also called the technical program, lasting 2 minutes or 2 minutes and 40 seconds, including required moves such as 3 jumps, 3 spins, and 2 sequences of footwork.

spin

A twirling movement in a variety of positions, on either foot or both feet.

toe loop

A loop jump, assisted by a boost from behind from the other toe.

World Championships

Competition between national champions to determine the best skaters in the world, usually held in March.

COMPETITION RESULTS

AS AN AMATEUR

Year	Competition	Result
1977	U.S. National Championships	9th
1978	World Championships	11th
	U.S. National Championships	3rd
1979	Flaming Leaves	1st
	U.S. National Championships	4th
1980	Olympic Winter Games	5th
	World Championships	5th
	U.S. National Championships	3rd
1981	World Championships	1st
	U.S. National Championships	1st
	U.S. Eastern Championships	1st
	Skate America	1st
	U.S. National Sports Festival	1st
1982	World Championships	1st
	U.S. National Championships	1st
	U.S. Eastern Championships	1st
	Skate America	1st
	NHK Trophy*	1st
1983	World Championships	1st
	U.S. National Championships	1st
	U.S. Eastern Championships	1st
	Golden Spin of Zagreb	1st
1984	Olympic Winter Games	1st
	World Championships	1st
	U.S. National Championships	1st
	U.S. Eastern Championships	1st

*Given by the Japanese National
  Government Broadcasting Corp.

AS A PROFESSIONAL

Year	Competition	Result
1986	Nutrasweet World Pro. F. S. Championship	1st
1990	U.S. Open Pro. Skating Championships	1st
1991	Nutrasweet World Pro F. S. Championships	2nd
	Nutrasweet Challenge of Champions	4th
	U.S. Open Pro. Skating Championships	2nd
1993	Hershey's Kisses Pro Am	2nd
1994	Fox Rock 'n' Roll Championships	1st
	The Gold Championships	1st
1995	Canadian Professional Championships	2nd
	Legends of Figure Skating	1st
	The Gold Championships	3rd
	The Best of the Best	1st
	Fox Rock 'n' Roll Championships	1st
1996	Legends of Figure Skating	1st
	The Gold Championships	2nd

TOURS AND SHOWS

1968–	Bowling Green Ice Horizons Show
1980–	International Stars on Ice Show, Bowling Green
1984–86	Ice Capades
1986	Scott Hamilton America Tour
1987–96	Discover Card Stars on Ice
1990	Scott Hamilton and Friends, Bowling Green
1993	Skate the Dream, benefit for AIDS
1993–95	Skates of Gold I, II, III
1995	Rhapsody on Ice, with Brian Orser
1995	Halloween on Ice, with Nancy Kerrigan
1995, 96	Too Hot to Skate
1996	Tribute to Sergei Grinkov
1996	Three Masters on Ice
1996	Disney's Beauty and the Beast

AWARDS AND HONORS

1981–84	U.S. Olympic Committee Athlete of the Year
1983	ISIA (Ice Skating Institute of America) Man of the Year Award
1984	Southland Olympia Award, for achievement and support of the amateur ideal
1985	Honorary Alumnus Award from Bowling Green State University for service and support
1986	Professional Skater of the Year Award
1987	Olympic Spirit Award, USOC, most ideal athlete of the 1984 Olympics
1988	Jacques Favert Award, International Skating Union
1990	U. S. Olympic Hall of Fame
1990	World Figure Skating Hall of Fame
1991	Crown Royal Achievement Award, given to athletes who have overcome problems
1993	Spirit of Giving Award, U.S. Figure Skating Association, for giving back to the USFSA
1994	F. Ritter Shumway Award, USFSA, for dedication and contributions
1994	Honorary Doctorate from BGSU
1996	Footprints in USFSC Figure Skating Walk of Fame

For Further Reading

About Skaters

Browning, Kurt, and Neil Stevens. **Kurt: Forcing the Edge**. Toronto: Harper Collins, 1991.

Burakoff, Alexis. **On the Ice**. Newton, MA: Hare & Hatter Books, 1994.

Donahue, Shiobhan. **Kristi Yamaguchi: Artist on Ice**. Minneapolis: Lerner, 1993.

Faulkner, Margaret. **I Skate!** Boston: Little Brown, 1979.

Gordeeva, Ekaterina, and E.M. Swift. **My Sergei: A Love Story**. New York: Warner Books, 1996.

Hilgers, Laura. **Great Skates**. Boston: Little Brown, 1991.

Orser, Brian, and Steve Milton. **Orser: A Skater's Life**. Toronto: Key Porter Books, 1988.

Sanford, William, and Carl Green. **Dorothy Hamill**. Parsippany, NJ: Crestwood House, 1993.

Savage, Jeff. **Kristi Yamaguchi: Pure Gold**. New York: Dillon Press, 1993.

Shaughnessy, Linda. **Elvis Stojko: Skating From the Blade**. Parsippany, NJ: Silver Burdett Press, 1998.

_____.**Michelle Kwan: Skating Like the Wind**. Parsippany, NJ: Silver Burdett Press, 1998.

_____.**Oksana Baiul: Rhapsody on Ice**. Parsippany, NJ: Silver Burdett Press, 1998.

About Skating

Indiana-World Skating Academy. **Figure Skating: Sharpen Your Skills**. Indianapolis: Masters Press, 1995.

Milton, Steve. **Skate: 100 Years of Figure Skating**. Toronto: Key Porter Books, 1996.

Sheffield, Robert, and Richard Woodward. **The Ice Skating Book**. New York: Universe Books, 1980.

Smith, Beverley. **Figure Skating: A Celebration**. Toronto: McClelland & Stewart, 1994.

Van Steenwyk, Elizabeth. **Illustrated Skating Dictionary for Young People**. New York: Harvey House, 1979.

Stories About Skating

Dodge, Mary M. **Hans Brinker or the Silver Skates**. Sisters, OR.: Questar, 1993.

Lowell, Melissa. Silver Blades series: **Breaking the Ice** (1993); **Competition** (1994); **Going for the Gold** (1994); **In the Spotlight** (1993). New York: Bantam.

Streatfeild, Noel. **Skating Shoes**. New York: Dell, 1982.

INDEX